CSU Poetry Series VI

NORTH SEA

by
Mark Jarman

Cleveland State University Poetry Center

ACKNOWLEDGMENTS

Some of these poems have appeared or will appear in the following publications, to which grateful acknowledgment is made.

ALEMBIC: From a Picture Book; What the Scriptures Tell Us; The Crossing; History

AMERICAN POETRY REVIEW: A Ghost Story

AMERICAN REVIEW: Powers That Be in This Neighborhood

ANTAEUS: Father, Son, and Ghost

THE CHOWDER REVIEW: We Dare Not Go A-Hunting

FIELD: Dead Reckoning; My Parents Have Come Home Laughing; At Sea; False Subjects; Required Mysteries

THE IOWA REVIEW: Planting; Premonition

KAYAK: In Sickness and Health; Lullaby for Amy

THE NATION: Kicking the Candles Out

THE NORTH AMERICAN REVIEW: Foreigners

POETRY: Goodbye to a Poltergeist; The Same Clay

POETRY NORTHWEST: Writing for Nora; Three Gods Share Their Pastimes

POETRY NOW: Pet Marjorie

THREE RIVERS POETRY JOURNAL: Shepherd; Growing Quiet; Sedative

Mr. Jarman has also published a chapbook, *Tonight Is the Night of the Prom*, Three Rivers Press, 1974.

Cover Drawing by Thomas Bucher.

Copyright © 1978 by Mark Jarman

Manufactured in the United States of America

Library of Congress Catalog No. 78-67730
ISBN 0-914-946-13-7
Distributed by NACSCORP, Inc., Oberlin, Ohio, and by *Field*, Oberlin College, Oberlin, Ohio

To
James Van Wagoner

TABLE OF CONTENTS

I
Dead Reckoning 11
Foreigners 12
We Dare Not Go A-Hunting 13
Planting 15
The Close 16
Pet Marjorie 18
My Parents Have Come Home Laughing 20
Before You 21
A Ghost Story 23
Kicking the Candles Out 26
From a Picture Book 27
Hemispheres 29
What the Scriptures Tell Us 30
Goodbye to a Poltergeist 32
The Crossing 33

II
History 37
The Same Clay 40
Shepherd 42
Growing Quiet 44
Writing for Nora 45
Money 47
Turistas 48
Premonition 51
At Sea 52
Father, Son, and Ghost 54
Altar Calls 56
Powers That Be in This Neighborhood 58
False Subjects 60
Three Gods Share Their Pastimes 62
Sedative 64
In Sickness and Health 65
Required Mysteries 66
Lullaby for Amy 68

... ghosts must do again
What gives them pain.

W. H. Auden

I

DEAD RECKONING

It's not a flaw
Or anything you've ever touched this way
On the smooth globe,
This one spot in relief, in Scotland
On the North Sea.

It is a house.
The snow on its roof is filmy,
Like moth dust,
Too slight to be cold.
And the slate edge
Of the chimney top is so fine
It even draws
A little of your blood, which settles
In the garden, caught
On the tips of thorns.

You lived here once
Not choosing to
In winter, which was hard.
Now, to come to it again.
To have chosen to come to it again.

And you are caught in the garden,
Suddenly small
Among brambles. The chimney towers
Above you, the smoke rises,
And unlike blood, which heals because it is warm,
The snow, leaning
Against the lighted windows and thickening
On your skin, is very cold.

FOREIGNERS

Now, in the stone kitchen,
The open honey jar is clotted with wasps;
A thin breeze chills the house
But we keep the window open.

Now we can take a little
From this place, having got through our first winter here.

Nights when the walls of hollow cinder block
Poured dust down through themselves
And the chimney flues blew out their gags of newspaper,
All the lights went on; we hurried
To the living room and waited.

Next door, in white cardigan and sun hat,
The widow comes to the garden wall and leans
Awkwardly over. She shows us the chink
Where the wasps have stuck their nest.
She offers us a cup of plaster
To close it, which we take.

Her lips are full and blue,
Her fingernails blue. Though we think
Her heavy arms and face
Have strength, we wonder,
Watching the wasps hover near their sealed hive,
If she will live much longer
Or, at least, as long as we live here.

WE DARE NOT GO A-HUNTING

Children, here
We call this widow's soap,
This film of soot
On the tile grate,
And this flaw in the window glass
You can peak through
Like a needle's eye
We call the Devil's pupil —
See how it distorts
The garden. The border stones
Of the rosebed
Are thrush's anvils.
Listen, you can hear
The snail crack.
The bird will gobble
The soft insides.
It's just a bird.
But that wing beat raising
It above the chimneys
Has a name — nestling's hour
Or man fear;
It depends on your mood.
When your breath in your own house
Steams from cold
And the tinkers knock
On your back door
With dry pussy willows
Begging shoes,
We call it winter burdens.
Don't be afraid

To send them away.
Only birds fear them,
Dart from their sticks
And stones. They'll curse
You and you'll want
To track them to their camps —
Wasted, tin shack, smokey
Places on the town's edge.
Let them have their disrespect.
Where they live soot
Is only soot on their faces,
Their soap is lye,
And they have ugly, simple
Names for hunger.

PLANTING

We are playing what our friend played
On the sea cliff: not falling.
It's a game where we walk the peaked
Mortar. Embedded gravel nicks our shoe heels.
And the wall, like a walk you dream of
In a bad dream, stretches out
From the coal bin to the end of the garden.
We won't fall. It's rhubarb on one side,
A plaster vase of bulbs on the other.
The factory chimney smears a black chalk line down the sky.

The day that boy crawled above us,
Delicate as a lizard, up the pigeon-holed cliff,
Dark blue in his school blazer and shorts,
We watched till the castle keep at the top
Melted him in shadow. How could he have fallen?
As if a trick had occurred
Like a blue bush from a hat, we turned
Our cricked necks to catch the magic
And he was down. A rain of torn clay
Pattered around us on the wet sand.

So, we are careful, remembering mainly
The way he mastered a wall — he could do it.
When you fall, rhubarb crunches like sugar.
When I fall, the plaster vase shatters
And the bulbs that the widow kept warm all winter
Spill over flagstones, ready for planting.

THE CLOSE

This is a good road to climb,
If wind is rising with you.
Behind are the park and bomb shelter,
Shelled chestnuts and those
Still in their husks,
And the bright steps leading down.
My satchel creaks on my shoulders,
Making me feel their width,
How little they warm my neck.

What small steps I take
Against the wind, past the abbey door.
In the chancel the flags hang still,
Like old dresses, piecing apart.
Up ahead three roads meet
And the swing shift is coming so thickly
The men appear seamless.
Their faces exude holy oils, flammable —
But that is just twilight.

There I'm as good as home.
A woman cries, "I shouldn't wish it colder!"
And blows past toward the factory gates,
Stork-crooked into the smoke.
Torn posters slap at themselves,
Blues and yellows scabbed with paste.
A dustman challenges with his wide broom
Then offers candy in sticks like chalk.
I eat what I take.

Already I've said my first platitudes
For their balm and weightlessness.
A family, all in black wool,
Who asked me for streets
With names like rivers I'd read of,
Went off swearing they'd soon be home.
Their cheeks were the color of eggs
Held to candles. I said,
"You can take this way."
They answered, "That's where we came from."

Let me tell you, though, I got home.
There was wind in the close, as always,
Bearing down between wall top and roof top,
Untying sweet pea tendrils.
I rubbed my feet on the mat,
And voices, first sharp
Then forgetting themselves,
Bloomed around me in the warm kitchen.

PET MARJORIE

I write from memory.
You composed prayers,
A divine, a pouting
Girl who loved Jesus.
In the churchyard grass
The dew seeps down
On the heels of rain
And you kneel on your grave,
Stone on stone.

On the way to the park
We ran past you
To pick horse chestnuts.
We shoved knitting needles
Through them, strung
Twine through the punctures,
And played a game
In which one boy let
His chestnut dangle,
Another smashed it with his.

One great find,
Knotted and bulged like a fist,
Like a hunk of rock candy
Shattered when tapped
And its owner cried.
The winner remained intact;
There was no prize
But wholeness; the hardest
Were often smallest.

Swung for a few years
At the end of God's thumb,
Little mealy chestnut,
In rain after rain
I pity you.
I pity all children
Who die, leaving
Instead of their childhoods,
Small books of devotions.

MY PARENTS HAVE COME HOME LAUGHING

My parents have come home laughing
From the feast for Robert Burns, late, on foot;
They have leaned against graveyard walls,
Have bent double in the glittering frost,
Their bladders heavy with tea and ginger.
Burns, suspended in a drop, is flicked away
As they wipe their eyes, and is not offended.

What could offend him? Not the squeaking bagpipe
Nor the haggis which, when it was sliced, collapsed
In a meal of blood and oats
Nor the man who read a poem by Scott
As the audience hissed embarrassment
Nor the principal speaker whose topic
"Burns' View of Crop Rotation" was intended
For farmers, who were not present,
Nor his attempt to cover this error, reciting
The only Burns poem all evening,
"Nine Inch Will Please a Lady," to thickening silence.

They drop their coats in the hall,
Mother first to the toilet, then Father,
And then stand giggling at the phone
Debating a call to the States, decide no,
And the strength to keep laughing breaks
In a sigh. I hear, as their tired ribs
Press together, their bedroom door not close
And hear also a weeping from both of them
That seems not to be pain, and it comforts me.

BEFORE YOU

    for my sister Luanne, conceived in Scotland, born in America

Before you began there is all of time.
Who can be jealous of that? And there's this time
In a country you are tired of imagining.
The albums that rock in your lap, heavy as thresholds,
The mementos we guide your hands to
Are not yours. And the ghosts we raise
From an old, kept-frozen snow of talk —
How can you keep believing them?

We have to haunt you to believe ourselves.
The marquetry of Loch Marie fails us.
We must tell how the swans planed by us,
Doubling their necks; how a deer stumbled
At the base of Mount Shiloch, into our picnic,
Horn-cut across the chest. Memory
Is selfish. You are bewildered proof.

You flame for your own air, subside,
And are led among flying fish, up tracks folded
In moss, with a bird part owl, part lies,
And with our hands for wings, shadowing you
Back to a bedroom. You see what Mother saw, on her back,
That blue ceiling and her breath rising
From the cold bed, and feel what she and Father felt
As they hollowed your pulse in the cold.

Still, you think, holding yourself,
That before you there was nothing.
The Flying Scotsman is leaving for 1960.
Frost steams from its black barrel.
Its stainless letters cloud, and your face clouds
With a blush half heat, half fear.
Girders open before us,
"Like an aisle of madrone!" you say, "In California."
Like a bridge; what a bridge promises.

A GHOST STORY

    for Katie

Four years old, the snow heaped
On thin plates of ice, you stepped
Among mounded flower beds
Behind the house and found him.
The kilt of the Black Watch frozen
Between his legs, like a carving.
You touched him, you said, and walked home
Holding your breath.

I saw from the tall classroom windows
The smoke tumble from chimneys;
I memorized simple tables, hearing
You cry that his cheeks were black
And his waxed moustache
Bitten through.
We had met him one day
From our garden wall. At attention,
His tam flopped on his head,
He prodded his flowers
With his drum major's staff.
You went to him.

There was a corner of our room
Where a green smoke
Kindled itself every night.
It began like an eyelid
On a moth wing
Flicking a light bulb, the wing's

Shadow flaring up.
It comforted us, though at times
We thought we would die of it.
At least we knew it was there;
In the whole house, only that corner.

Then the drum major
Stood beside your bed, bending to kiss you.
He came every night for months
To your bed or to Mother and Father's
With you tucked between them.
The ice-sharpened hem of his kilt
Stroked you awake; his mouth
In its cold hairs shut yours.
The house was searched;
You were searched.

He slipped from the filaments
Of lights that burned all night,
In silence, not a clue.

We have not spoken of this
Since he stopped. Your age was blamed;
That country of ghosts.
You would narrow your eyes
And laugh. Ghosts are knots
A comb can tug through;
They are closet mirrors, cloudy hangers.

Your loom's warp is taut,
The cherry wood frame lucent

By the window with the Oregon weather.
Your hair slips across the shuttle;
Gets caught; you swear; and under
Your house the pump, choking,
Evacuates rain water.

2000 miles away,
Describing you by heart, from another time,
I know only that you're alive.

KICKING THE CANDLES OUT

I have sat below a platform in Scotland
In a cold room where Sunday school met
And overhead watched the men dancing,
Their thighs flexing the beat
Into their waists, their arms curled like antlers,
And their women, as good dancers as they,
As muscular and light, shouting.
Hours of music I can no longer hear
Keeps them sweeping their boot toes
So near the ceiling, with its cracks and rain-patches,
That they graze the lights hanging on chains,
Making them turn in a drizzle of plaster
Slowly as planets, and keeping them turning.

FROM A PICTURE BOOK

God save that sweet face!
Burn the hoor.

The spring is all sweetness,
The golden birches,
In country phrase,
Letting down their hair, bird-dizzy
In the Perthshire peaks.
They have talked long.
Horses sidle and snatch,
Their bits jingling, and hawks
Half-roused tug at their jesses.
Knox is aware of the Court's impatience
As the sun rising smokes mist off the hilltops
And Mary, mounted above him, bends
Flatteringly from the saddle.

Apparitional in her gesture
She recalls the Frenchman who taught her
Dances and fashions,
Who kissed a book of Ronsard
Calling her, as he knelt to the block,
La plus belle et cruelle princesse.
When the heart is caught,
Blood catches it.
To the holy, dour man beneath her,
Her open face to his,

Both of them gauging shrewdness,
She whispers some silly rumor.

For her hawks will collide
Tumbling through air
And Earl Bothwell pace a groove
In a cell floor in Denmark
And Knox comprehend political necessities.
Even as the hunting party rides on,
Scarletly, with bells, their own hearts
Caught by their beauty, their lady's crown
Is a quiver of spring light held steady,
Made solid, stubbornly hovering
Over James's head, in Knox's hands.

HEMISPHERES

He lifts me above a wave or a crowd
bracing my back and head like a baby's
and laughs. In California the sun
draws sweat from his forehead; in Scotland
the crowd surges like Pacific shallows.

He propels us against surf like shoulders,
people like caps of foam. At its stillest
a thin net of the ocean climbs so slowly
the beach leans like a mountain grade.
The whole swathe clings by a hem.

The Queen of England mounts the platform
I can see clearly from my father's arms, to applause,
the North Sea tilted behind her.
And the sand goes dark.
And the sand becomes pale again.

WHAT THE SCRIPTURES TELL US

> I would gladlie know what a black bible
> is that which is called, the Book of the wicked
>
> Z. Boyd, *Last Battell*

In the black bible, the wicked Book
we have only fragments,
all black.

Our eyes pierce the sunlight,
that suffusion that hates
the eye,

and each figure curled in our pupils
is a cool, focused black
fragment

we could look at forever.
Wicked or not, when it is here
night is familiar.

But to watch it begin, piece by piece,
how can we know it?

*

When we remember the growth
on the cat's hip, clam-shaped,
overnourished,

remember the stroke-victim asleep
whose arm rises, dreaming
of rising,

the black bible is open. For our sakes
it reads that memory is redemptive, that blood
is thicker than earth.

Think of it, the health of the mind,
the Book of the wicked laid
on the pillow,

ending the nightmare,
ending dreams that, on waking, we wish
to return to,

ending sleep altogether.

*

Always, when we still want to see
as if we stood at a picture window
comparing the view to scenes in a guidebook,
birds, hundreds of them, beat the glass
smearing it with the oil of their feathers,
black birds, breaking through sunlight.

GOODBYE TO A POLTERGEIST

Like an empty socket alone
On a long baseboard, nothing connects
With him anymore. The bundled family
Has tramped away with its suitcases.
In the spots where he hid he finds light.
To him the dust, with nothing to settle on,
Is a dreary rain.

His push-and-pull with the household gods
Is over; his own knocking rattles him.
His squatter's rights continue but how
To assert them with no one living to gibber at,
No sleeping ear to enter
Or hot brain to poach his eye, the nightmare?

Perhaps, he never existed.
Perhaps, with new residents he will find himself
No longer himself; some unfamiliar dampness
Under a bed will expel him,
A fresh draft blow him deep between floorboards.
He is slowly unfolding, like a crumpled paper
Left in a closet, inanimately with a faint creak.

He needs the children who lived here, who are now
Releasing rolls of streamers from a boatside.
What a mess of tape as the bright wheels unspin
And the boat is tugged out.
In their minds, his rooms, his house, his drizzle of dust
In the cleansing light are cut to ribbons
And sink like ribbons, absorbed by the air.

THE CROSSING

You taught me to say goodbye
The way your fingers on mine
Taught me to slice and eat,
To button and unbutton.

The undertow of your voice
Was taking us away,
Veering near the North Pole.
I got the hang of it.

I saw how we would go
By the stitch points of your belly,
How the cracked skin of California
Would close, forgetting us.

How did I learn all that?
I was six. The North Atlantic
Was a story you told
That came true, page after page.

The waves unimpressed with us,
Churning to end farewells —
I remember the waves.
Or did you tell me that, too?

Our first cold night in Scotland
Your nightgown rode to your hips
And Father aimed for the heat,
The adhering heat.

I remember, but I was asleep.
Who is speaking here, Mother?

I can't break you from me
As I was cut from you,

Though we were both removed
With a guard rope caught in both hands
And the ocean tilting in reach,
Leaving and returning.

II

HISTORY

I

They're all drunk tonight in the old country,
my Welsh and Norman fathers tipping
pitchers of warm wine. In a field where evening dampens
dried blood, the palm-oiled table
creates another kind of pain.
A French name is soon to lose
its scented, nasal moisture. Charlemagne —
bread from a jug of milk squeezed and seared
and broken in the mouth — Jarman. The drowsy moan.
Between their sons and daughters bone is forged,
the opposing tongues are blended.

II

The cattle-thieving brothers were shipped away.
One tumbled overboard with a green face, one
disappeared in calm weather, the other three
rocked with the creaking, pitch-blended timbers
and made it.

And had to make new strangers with stranger names
know theirs. First, on the damp sand where they smoldered.
And then, every day: the difficult timbre of splitting syllables
in America; three men without a roof stretching one name
to cover them all.

I see one of them turn toward me now,
bitter, irreligious,
wielding a branch too thick for whipping children.
I know I know that mouth, ordering, "Go!
Make your own name for yourself."

III
The God of Missouri
said to a girl that that man she loved
with the odd beautiful name
would clothe and feed her,
that she must teach him as he slept
and ate, mix God with his bread,
God with her sex cries,
and alliterate that man's name with Jesus
till his skull cracked with The Light.

And I know what she did.
Clothed and fed by him,
she said "Jarman" and "Jesus"
till both words cracked together
and her husband could not be made
to eat or sleep or stop babbling.
And she accepted this sacrifice.
And the Spirit got into the family name.

IV
My uncles and fathers have serious business,
they won't stop prodding the coals.
The picnic has lasted till after dark.
Each in turn, with glowing skewers,
they describe divine plans for the family,
how to get Heaven on earth.
They pray for their business partners, the children.

Such evenings break off late
with a half-whispered hymn, children whining,
and alone by the dull fire,
controlling their voices, Father and Grandfather
too much in each other's bad dreams,
sending one another to Hell.

In the back seat, asleep, driving home,
a child who heard some
holiness in the leaves
say his name, and crossed his eyes at the moon,
does not dream he will ever deny
his only world, but he will.

V

In a small house in Greater Los Angeles, six blocks from the ocean, I don't remember what year, after I shamed my parents in church with some childish sacrilege and they scolded me — this happened, perhaps, because I wanted it to happen: sun-glare burst like surf into my room, waves pinned me to the floor, and I heard a grinding — it was my name being powdered like a shell. As the light slowly withdrew, it took my name, the last sounds of it dissolving into the future. When it was all over, of course I still knew who I was. And I knew something else, just as important. I knew what I wanted for the rest of my life and what I did not want. I wanted my name to have a meaning of utmost secrecy. I did not want ever to mistake my identity for the one my family gave me.

Now, I have met a woman who has lost her name in mine and for her, as a kind of sacrifice, I do not want sons, but daughters who may someday lose their names. This is the logic, I know, of a child who believed his name could be magical. It is also his selfishness — no one will keep my name after me. Thinking of that, I can hardly sleep. I hear my parents imploring me: your name includes you with us, they say; we know you are Mark Jarman. The future stuns me. The waves peak and dissolve. What I wanted I will have and not need. And what I did not want, and lost, I will want back again.

THE SAME CLAY

You have it in Oregon
where white lumber rolls up on
the beaches and agates are

pried by fingernail out of
the clay cliffs, that nothing here,
except under snow, is so

memorable. You are sure,
for we have assured you, that,
returning, we will forget

all but the first time we woke
to cities and fields of snow.
That was one morning. Others

before when our one window
was stuck with leaves, or since, as
trees have begun to break out

and earth to split open, green,
are moments we've seen better
at home. As for forgetting,

the days here, less precious but
harder than agates, are lodged
in the same clay as our days

there, but firmer; each one we'd
rather forget is sunk deep
as pain, resisting all pressure,

maintaining its crystal edge.
Furthermore, when we return
we have no way of knowing

which of the great lengths of time
that have passed and will pass here
will, eventually, wash

into the lives we resume
there, bleached by amnesia,
gigantic, immoveable.

SHEPHERD

No prayers tonight for the separate
soul, that fume
under pressure in the body.
Above are the constellations
dismembered by haze
and the sparse offering
plate of the moon.

The suburban pastor on his lawn,
robed and careful
among the gopher mounds,
makes a motion like a sprinkler.
It's warm, the Basin stirred
by ghosts of river breezes,
the true Pacific.

He sees the image of his pulpit,
crumpled ice ship,
and the image of the glacial pews
crack in diminishing halves
sinking end up.

Moths form
a fuzzy chandelier
around the porch light.
Body is an orbiter
and soul a sun —
but not tonight.

Jowl gray as the dawn,
grass blades sparking

under bare feet,
he prays for his flock
of emptinesses, the gopher holes,
each filled, and those
small skulls filled
like his own with light.

Stars are settling
among houses as workers rise
and pairs of headlights
along the lost streets
begin finding, finding
his blessing follows them
over hills.

GROWING QUIET

When did the mumbling begin?
Your speech become the gesture
of a fist pushing down
through a pocket?

Was it a moment too cold
for your tongue? A cube of pain
still clamped between
your back teeth?

What does the bright blind linoleum
read and the lawn and the sidewalk
as the syllables drop from your lips
like wads of paper in secret?

In the hum of your head
the unmuffled answers must
beat and beat. We can hear
your joints crack in time.

If you would speak like
the earth bound in stone
we could hear the pressure
and know how deep how much.

Drawn back in a brooding
corner, your voice is a pulse
losing touch. We hear only
how quiet you're growing.

WRITING FOR NORA

I should be pleasing myself, you know,
old woman, though I owe
myself to you. Through the hospital window
edged with ferns, the trucks and birds appear,
gearing up hill, up air.
Should they be included?
They have not been informed you are here.
Or that I, waiting with you
for your last seizure, can't
stand to listen again
as your dictaphone winds through
the summer of the first:
the buckets of sweet water,
the sponges stroking and stroking,
your wrists and ankles cinched
because your prone dancing tore
too many sheets ... Each time I've almost
got it, the red
recording tape ticks off
and again you accuse me,
thinking me one of the brothers who sent you to fetch
foxfire in the woods, and followed, and watched,
laughing when you fell down.
I can't convince you they are gone.
Bold as the girl
you think you are you twirl
around in bed and thrust your knees
in my face,
pointing to scars as fresh cuts,
to the shine of the loose skin.

Desperate story-teller,
those words of yours that wore me out
sworn on tapes crammed in a box
will be lost.
You know I owe you them.
And you will twist
me everywhere to find, at least,
one way to tell how you died
the way you would tell it, digressions turning
and twisting till I fall
as you fell in your fit,
Grandmother, ghost, epileptic,
caught, sick of it.

MONEY

That woman who escorts the child
to the corner as she did this winter,
out of sight, smoking, returning

in late afternoon knows no change.
Her hair is the same sponge from undersea,
gray, spined. Her child

with brown bag and covered books
sits at evening behind a screen
of pink tea roses

on the smokey porch toward the sun,
not hungry in any event.
Their poverty is our empty onlooking,

which is blameless
as dogs in a gang with smiling moustaches,
every bird's courtesy, leaves complimenting

faces at windows, silver bellies
turned by wind,
the green, bouyant weather of a tree's

afternoon, like gin
poured by a host whose budget
is the whole season.

Across the yard, blurred now
as the dead jay under the peony bush,
our lit windows creep toward each other

and our shadows in the windows,
looking at ourselves
looking, poor and apart.

TURISTAS

The mosquitoes have a taste for me
you don't. They've been descending
from some corner of the ceiling,
each to make its mark and fill.
They take no more
than enough, then rise to the lamp.
Some become blood samples on the wall.
I'm caught between my fascination
for their humming and your silence.

It's Mazatlan, 1966,
and I have asked for too much.
You've turned the shower in my path.
Huddled as if to shield
a child, you are a child, having thought
till now I was as much
your sister as your brother. In the streets
our parents price wicker and onyx.
I wait for the water to cool.

Fourteen and twelve,
we've waited out the summer.
We drove past
a man shaking a guitar for sale
with mother-of-pearl winking on its neck.
He saw our parents shake their heads.
Waggling his tongue like a finger,
he saw my hand between your knees.

What a coolness we radiated!
Mother and Father in front,
like a team of horses, and the clouds
in the mountains level with us.
Except where thighs touched
we were cool and dry.

One afternoon we got drunk
on fumes of chlorine, rising
and falling in the motel pool
until our eyes were bloody.
A swimming beetle reached for us.
We took our hands away,
slapped the water into froth and flung it out,
then could not touch each other.

These images, hovering
and attacking, end as flecks of blood.
You remind me of Mother,
water-sick in traffic,
gripping the map,
crying all day into Mexico's
crooked spine.

You've held your pose so long!
Driving the coastal desert,
you'd put my hands aside, smiling,
and in the mountains let them lie.
That's all behind us. The spray's lukewarm
but still a barrier. Weak, we lean
toward each other trembling the way

some children we saw trembled, slipping
off their shirts by a flooded ditch.
Too hot to mind
they dove in and churned
the white and yellow scum like a sea.
Perhaps, tonight they can't breathe
or they're well, happy to be foolish
just as we are unhappy, and well,
and still you will not have me.

PREMONITION

Mother, I see you blocking the door,
your skin is a mesh of light
letting the night through,
your breasts are no longer toylike
as in the bath, they are cones
of moonlight tipped with darkness,
and between your thighs
that reddish wedge of hair
that hovered near my palm-sized face
is white with a black crease.

When you turn completely to memory
that is the shape you'll take,
reminding me each time I pass
through you into another room
that death is a short trip;
your heart stops and you're there.

AT SEA

I remember someone saying once
— who'd never seen the ocean —
that the skin rubbed from the drowned
flames coldly there at night.
This boat has been my bed
and table now for days
and I've seen that fire
but there's a warmth about it.
Somehow, like a hearth,
it makes me feel at home.
I think I could go on
holding on like this for life.

*

I do get scared sometimes,
illusions billow toward me;
they can be touched. I shake
my father's hand and we observe
the weather. The distance we maintain
is natural, the wind that slams
between us like a door
is not. A wave will fall
and there will be my wife walking
as if back to bed asleep, or
she will not be there. The waves will fold
back, and nothing will be there.

*

Of course, the calms are the worst.
I think I am some useless,
fourlimbed fish, dangling
my arms between my knees.
I don't believe in land;
water, if it took me back,
would cripple me. I've rocked
myself like this before,
once outside a bedroom
where I knew death was working,
humming a little to calm myself
because it was too calm.

*

Lately, I'm less certain.
Though I wake up always knowing
where I am, really
I don't know. I lie letting the sun
blister me as I sleep.
I stare all night at the moon.
I was sure the current under me
would grow colder, slower,
like a bloodstream running
too far from the heart, that all
of this would end, and it continues.

FATHER, SON, AND GHOST

The day I am baptized
the blind man with a little silver box
takes me aside.
I know his trick.
The dead man's finger
knuckle up on black silk,
tapping, twitching, is his
but I see a woman's
white-nailed and still,
and he shows me his free hands.

My father waits with hip boots on,
his robe puffed up around him
on the water, and nothing up
his loose, black, baggy sleeves.
Empty, the tin sides of the baptistry
boom when you step in,
now they're taut as skins.
With a hold he knows and water's
help he can bewilder gravity,
and tips me back.

Already I can taste the flakey
bread pellet, the grape juice,
and see myself replacing
the thimble cup in the felt pew ring.
All secrets are one secret
the underwater seems to say,

and when I rise the white
face of the blind man
rises above the baptistry edge,
grinning as I gasp.

No revelation comes.
Water draining from my ears
leaves a weak, denying voice
I've heard for months, which tells
over and over the story
of a man who lost his congregation
by asking as he raised them,
blinking, from the water, what they saw.
I saw my father had a broken tooth,
my ten fingers closed around his hand.

ALTAR CALLS

I know what it means when
my father's jaw tightens.
He is hearing his father scorn
his first prayers. When he wakes
he knows night after night
the dream will not change.

Sometimes I know why
my father hated his, at the table
as brass collection plates
catch light, and the underglow
in my grandfather's face
shifts like water.

I watch the two of them
for what fathers and sons can become.
They stand at the heads of their congregations
with different prayers in their mouths,
complex as ferns, eyes tilted toward rafters,
knowing better.

When the new family comes forward
they extend the hand they never offered each other.
When the child confesses
they lower him into water
with an embrace they save
for that moment.

I hear in the underbreath
of my own prayer the wish
they hear in theirs:

"Bless what I offer
without tearing it from my hands."
We do not know better.

I can almost tell
when my father remembers his mother's
ashes, how he learned
they were sealed in his father's church fountain.
Fifteen years later, led there
he did not ask to be left alone.

POWERS THAT BE IN THIS NEIGHBORHOOD

Voice within the whirlwind,
there's a nasal twang in the air —
song of the lady spraying
plant food at her lilacs,
cries of the young family in the street
knocking a whiffle ball around —
the yard of dobermans next door
can't stand it, the bushes
crash and growl. And a jet
rumbling in overhead, peace
making, crushes the sound.

Eyes above the overcast,
while the lady squints at
the film on heartshaped leaves,
and the whiffle ball hangs in its arc
as the family scurries beneath,
and the dogs guard
the ground between their paws,
a pigeon struggles to perch
in the dry shag of a palm tree
where its mate — the tiny red
beads in its head showing nothing —
clutches a leaf and looks on.

Hands below the paving,
the cracked sidewalk sprinkled
with pigeon dirt and feathers
and the white street veined
with tar are slowly shifting,

while under the knees of the lady
with her face buried in lilacs,
under the sturdy soles
of the family playing ball,
under the dogs' claws
the earth packed with wires
and plumbing is slowly shifting.

Powers that be in this neighborhood,
every day you walk through,
nodding hello, or roar in
over the palm trees. Will the smell
of lilacs never smother the lady?
Will the plastic ball never
blow the young family to pieces?
Will the dogs never swallow
their fierceness? Every day,
the blank look of the pigeon,
the flexing of stones under concrete,
the blue silence above the overcast,
the answers you have always given.

FALSE SUBJECTS

> Wondrous the Gods more wondrous are the Men
> More Wondrous Wondrous still the Cock & Hen
>
> Wm Blake

The sea, for one, the oily promoter, a caption
for itself blown larger than itself.

And the irksome meddling with parents
who live quietly, now, without us.

And our own conventional, shopworn bodies,
arks of misinformation, bald lies.

Even to think of them, to name them,
provokes a shudder urging think again!

Crabs in a coffee can are true,
kept in a chest of drawers, stinking.

And the dignified restraint of Mother and Father,
saving it for privacy, was true enough.

And how true the cysts, the pale strips
of healed skin, pocks, pores, and the bitter eyes.

How exactly the mica bit of wing evokes
the fly, and the fly the loop of shit.

The sea gloms onto the earth, in the distance.
Our parents are such mammoths, impossible.

And our bodies — sleep, dream, they are useless.
But salt, a closed door, a wart

are particles, particulars, single notes suggesting
single notes, our true and lasting concerns.

THREE GODS SHARE THEIR PASTIMES

Neptune

"You want to see death up close? See a mouth
so empty the sea has to fill it?
Through the telescope, drowning
is like the dying of a cell —
that magnified, that curious and small.
Where you stand you can pick the horizon apart,
bring a freighter to your eye, with its crawling deck,
and when the reef crumples the hull
and the deck spills — here you are to see it."

His house was a box of glass,
cool as lichen,
stilted above the Pacific. He said, "Remember,
when you look through the telescope
if you see death and forget what you see,
think of your eyes under coins,
think of death's metal lenses."

Mercury

"When I stretch out on the grass,
no one can call me. The light fades,
increasing in some other sky,
and my body lessens,
is less to imagine.
When the stars appear, I remember
I could span the distance
to each, propelling myself
with one thought, if I wanted to think it."

His caduceus lay by his side
like a double helix unravelled.
He said, "The stars are relaxing. Join me.
Near death the minutes pass
just as they pass after life.
How much time do you think we could kill,
lying here, counting them?"

Vulcan

"I was given a woman.
I said I could hammer my own
from sheet metal, but
I was given this woman.
She leaves, every day,
for the world of her own powers.
I can see her there, making
the blood come to men's faces,
the taste of smoke in her mouth."

He was pouring molten lead into water,
watching the metal clench.
He said, "All day, in my mind,
I follow her. When she comes home,
my hands are clean, glistening with lotion.
She expects me to take her.
I do not. I sit and watch her."

SEDATIVE

The birds that ruin nests
are asleep, and the worst dogs
slouched against curbs, whimpering.
The night is fairly safe
for the pet let out only at dark.
In her pit of silk, the patio
spider squats, content, as
I am, with the evening so far.

Earlier, suspicion and brooding
— paternal uncles — visited.
They don't approve of my life:
these rooms where love is a constant
threat aren't small enough;
the weather is bad, which is good,
but at night with windows black
I seem to forget, and relax.

I seem to relax; guilt,
my father, who lives with his brothers,
was forgotten as the windows darkened.
Now there's a white thing
quivering in the spider's lap.
Now there's my wife calling
from her own sleep into mine
that sleep is a pit. I can't help it.

IN SICKNESS AND HEALTH

Remember the pylons, the plateaus of concrete,
and the earth like a cracked casing,
seeping a dye of buds and pollen
all during that sickness; each glass of water
that stood overnight, the bubbles of air
like stars or fish eggs, the chalk taste
of drinking the pond full of fever.

Remember fever, a smear on the windows,
the fear that the last blunt icicle
that shrank in your sleep was money melting;
as the harboring blankets peeled away
and the city shrugged out of hiding,
how health, clear-eyed, sweating,
wanted too much to hold you again.

Remember, she was health; she is.
Hating these walls, she endured
their breath and yours, every day,
as long as she could. Hating this city,
she returned to your room with fresh sick-clothes.
She filled that glass by your bed
with the last cup of clean snow. Now help her.

She kneels in the living room filling it
with a cry, an embarrassing loneliness.
There is nothing silly to dance about.
The crease of your undershirt on her face
channels tears. There is nothing to laugh at.
You are well again. You are hers.
You have married the patient wait for exhaustion.

REQUIRED MYSTERIES

My body must be fitted to them.
Chimneys and the smell of smoked fish,
too, are the brain's light.
My hand pokes from a sleeve
covered with raspberry stains.
I can hold it before me only
an instant; it's bored; it reaches elsewhere.

I can force others to form
like smoke caught in a jar.
In the kitchen, Mother
stirs a jam pot, muffled;
the steam reddens her blurred hands.
Outside it is either of the year's
two weathers: grayness or cold sunlight,
and the window is a page of frost.

All light. The bed to be made
in mid sea among effigies.
There are two seeings within,
both spring like a trap
from the usualness of one moment
to struggle, to limp, squinting.

One thing will not be fixed.
Light pushes off from it
or slips past it; it is not
without its visionary pattern
like a potato in its earth
or the pale celery heart of red rhubarb,

but nakeder. It's a girl,
half concerned, pleased to be naked
and unseen, to stand away
from the brambles, the bracken, sure of herself,
exhausting my quick turns and fakes;
like everything I have not remembered,
frantically happy that she could
be come upon and won't be.

LULLABY FOR AMY

We are here, in another provisional city,
talking of places we will live.
Our bed is another world inside
the blocks of Midwestern houses,
the windows each showing the moon
of a streetlight through Chinese blinds,
watery reflections on the walls,
tropical and bland.
The way birds follow weather
we followed circumstance
and wait for it to change.

The earth is a wave that will not set us down.

Last summer our nerves lay down
to sleep a month in the mountains.
One night in two hours of rain
the river, far below us, rose
around its islands of motels.
A man on the road was picked up
off his feet, an old couple
was torn with him, fanned out
with others thirty miles away.
Cars bobbed with headlights on,
shuddered and ducked under.

The earth is a wave that will not set us down.

There is a town in Scotland
on the edge of the North Sea. In fall
the carnival unbolts its haywire rides
along the strand. Night sweeps in
from Norway with the breath of cod;
candles are set afloat in wash tubs.

With a leaky water gun you snuff three wicks
and win a coconut. I hear the screams
of prizewinners, smell the cod
on slabs in the High Street markets.
Sixteen years. I have never been back.

The earth is a wave that will not set us down.

Or does wherever we sleep become our home?
I see us walking among castles
that are great mounds and windings
of wet sand, in the mist of waves
breaking out of sight.
Like the horn of a lost boat,
a voice says, "Live here
as you used to live."
And it surprises us, so that we stop
and look back at our scar of footprints,
for we have always lived here, in this way.